VOLUME 8
SUPERHEAVY

BATMAN

D1157829

# BATMAN

## VOLUME 8
## SUPERHEAVY

WRITTEN BY
**SCOTT SNYDER**

PENCILS BY
**GREG CAPULLO**

INKS BY
**DANNY MIKI**

COLOR BY
**FCO PLASCENCIA**

LETTERS BY
**STEVE WANDS**

INTERLUDE
WRITTEN BY
**SCOTT SNYDER
& BRIAN AZZARELLO**

ART BY
**JOCK**

COLORS BY
**LEE LOUGHRIDGE**

LETTERS BY
**DERON BENNETT**

COLLECTION COVER ARTISTS
**GREG CAPULLO
& DANNY MIKI**

BATMAN CREATED BY
**BOB KANE** with **BILL FINGER**
SUPERMAN CREATED BY
**JERRY SIEGEL & JOE SHUSTER**
BY SPECIAL ARRANGEMENT WITH
THE JERRY SIEGEL FAMILY

MARK DOYLE Editor – Original Series
REBECCA TAYLOR Associate Editor – Original Series
DAVE WIELGOSZ  MATT HUMPHREYS Assistant Editors – Original Series
JEB WOODARD Group Editor – Collected Editions
ROBIN WILDMAN Editor – Collected Edition
STEVE COOK Design Director – Books
DAMIAN RYLAND Publication Design

BOB HARRAS Senior VP – Editor-in-Chief, DC Comics

DIANE NELSON President
DAN DIDIO and JIM LEE Co-Publishers
GEOFF JOHNS Chief Creative Officer
AMIT DESAI Senior VP – Marketing & Global Franchise Management
NAIRI GARDINER Senior VP – Finance
SAM ADES VP – Digital Marketing
BOBBIE CHASE VP – Talent Development
MARK CHIARELLO Senior VP – Art, Design & Collected Editions
JOHN CUNNINGHAM VP – Content Strategy
ANNE DEPIES VP – Strategy Planning & Reporting
DON FALLETTI VP – Manufacturing Operations
LAWRENCE GANEM VP – Editorial Administration & Talent Relations
ALISON GILL Senior VP – Manufacturing & Operations
HANK KANALZ Senior VP – Editorial Strategy & Administration
JAY KOGAN VP – Legal Affairs
DEREK MADDALENA Senior VP – Sales & Business Development
JACK MAHAN VP – Business Affairs
DAN MIRON VP – Sales Planning & Trade Development
NICK NAPOLITANO VP – Manufacturing Administration
CAROL ROEDER VP – Marketing
EDDIE SCANNELL VP – Mass Account & Digital Sales
COURTNEY SIMMONS Senior VP – Publicity & Communications
JIM (SKI) SOKOLOWSKI VP – Comic Book Specialty & Newsstand Sales
SANDY YI Senior VP – Global Franchise Management

BATMAN VOL. 8: SUPERHEAVY

Published by DC Comics. Compilation and all new material Copyright © 2016 DC Comics. All Rights Reserved.

Originally published in single magazine form in BATMAN 41-45 and online as DC SNEAK PEEK: BATMAN 1 Copyright © 2015 DC Comics. All Rights Reserved. All characters, their distinctive likenesses and related elements featured in this publication are trademarks of DC Comics. The stories, characters and incidents featured in this publication are entirely fictional. DC Comics does not read or accept unsolicited submissions of ideas, stories or artwork.

DC Comics, 2900 West Alameda Avenue, Burbank, CA 91505
Printed by RR Donnelley, Salem, VA, USA. 8/5/16. First Printing.
ISBN: 978-1-4012-6630-1

Names: Snyder, Scott, author. | Capullo, Greg, illustrator. | Miki, Danny,
illustrator. | Plascencia, Fco, illustrator. | Wands, Steve, illustrator.
| Azzarello, Brian, author. | Jock, 1972- illustrator. | Loughridge, Lee,
illustrator. | Bennett, Deron, illustrator.
Title: Batman. Volume 8, Superheavy / written by Scott Snyder ; pencils by
Greg Capullo ; inks by Danny Miki ; colors by Fco Plascencia ; letters by
Steve Wands ; INTERLUDE written by Scott Snyder and Brian Azzarello ; art
by Jock ; colors by Lee Loughridge ; letters by Deron Bennett ; collection
cover by Greg Capullo and Danny Miki.
Other titles: Superheavy
Description: Burbank, CA : DC Comics, [2016]
Identifiers: LCCN 2015049450 | ISBN 978-1-4012-6630-1
Subjects: LCSH: Graphic novels. | Superhero comic books, strips, etc. |
BISAC: COMICS & GRAPHIC NOVELS / Superheroes.
Classification: LCC PN6728.B36 S689 2016 | DDC 741.5/973—dc23
LC record available at http://lccn.loc.gov/2015049450

PEFC Certified

Printed on paper from
sustainably managed
forests and controlled
sources

PEFC™
PEFC/29-31-75    www.pefc.org

"YOU SEE IT AND YOU *KNOW* JUST WHAT IT MEANS.

"IT MEANS *HE'S* COMING.

"IT APPEARS IN THE SKY AND IMMEDIATELY YOU CAN SENSE IT, SENSE HIM ON HIS WAY...

"...YOU CAN *HEAR* THE RUMBLE OF THE CAR. *SEE* THE GROWING SHADOW...

"...YOU'RE SMILING WITHOUT KNOWING IT. A TINGLING IN YOUR HANDS.

"YOU FEEL HIS APPROACH LIKE A SONG INSIDE YOU, DARK AND JOYFUL, SWELLING, THE SAME NOTES OVER AND OVER, LIKE A DRUMBEAT GETTING FASTER.

"NA. NA. NA-NA, NA-NA-NA-NA..."

"WELL, PERHAPS-- MERCIFULLY--THANKS TO *ONE* GOTHAM INSTITUTION, WE *WON'T* HAVE TO FIND OUT.

"FOR NEARLY THREE CENTURIES, *POWERS INTERNATIONAL* HAS BEEN ONE OF THE MOST *PROMINENT* CORPORATE CITIZENS OF GOTHAM CITY, AND THE NATION.

"NOW, WITH THEIR *ACQUISITION* OF THE RECENTLY *DEFUNCT* WAYNE ENTERPRISES, THE POWERS FAMILY IS LOOKING TO *BROADEN* THEIR ROLE IN THE CITY'S RECONSTRUCTION. FROM RESIDENTIAL PROJECTS TO MUNICIPAL SITES...

13

GOTHAM NEWS 13  Powers International: "Time to start over"...**GOTHAM NEWS 13**

"...TO *BATMAN* HIMSELF."

## CEO GERI POWERS

THERE IS NO REPLACING BATMAN. THE MAN WHO INSPIRED US, WHO FOUGHT AND DIED PROTECTING US...HE'LL *ALWAYS* BE THE GREATEST HERO THIS CITY HAS EVER KNOWN.

BUT THE FACT IS, THIS CITY *NEEDS* A BATMAN. WE BELIEVE THAT HERE. *I* BELIEVE IT, DEEPLY AND TRULY. I DIDN'T ALWAYS...UNTIL WE LOST HIM, AND NOW I DO.

AND WHILE THERE'S NO REPLACING THE ORIGINAL BATMAN, MAYBE THERE'S A WAY TO *HONOR* HIM, BY CARRYING ON HIS WORK IN A *NEW* WAY.

SO HERE AT POWERS, WE'VE BEEN WORKING WITH THE MAYOR'S OFFICE, WITH THE CITY GOVERNMENT, EVEN WITH THE

"THERE IS A SECRET CORNER OF NATURE WE'RE ONLY NOW JUST DISCOVERING.

"A DARK AND HIDDEN SECTION OF THE PERIODIC TABLE.

"IT'S FULL OF MYSTERIOUS NEW ELEMENTS. MATERIAL *BEYOND* OUR REACH...UNTIL NOW. STRANGE AND *GLOWING* WITH POSSIBILITY.

"THESE ELEMENTS ONLY EXIST FOR A *MOMENT,* A FLASH OF ATOMIC COLLISION BENEATH GOTHAM--AND THEN THEY VANISH.

"IN THAT MOMENT, WE HAVE TO DETERMINE--IT'S OUR *RESPONSIBILITY* TO DETERMINE--ARE THESE NEW THINGS WONDROUS..."

"...IT."

Ah, I bet I know what you're thinking.

Yes, you.

You're thinking, the signal is supposed to shine **up** into the sky. Not down at the ground.

But then again, why **not**, right? Lately, it's almost like the whole city has been turned upside down.

Like it's been completely upended by Batman's death. Ever since--

AHEM. YOU'RE AWFULLY QUIET. TELL ME YOU'RE NOT NAVEL-GAZING AGAIN.

BATMAN HAS NO NAVEL.

WHAT'S THE SITUATION, JULIA?

WE'RE SEEING **ENERGY**, BATMAN. SOME KIND OF WALKING BIOELECTRIC FIELD. WHATEVER IT IS, IT'S TEARING UP LITTLE CUBA IN **THE NARROWS**.

SPECIFICALLY, IT SEEMS LIKE IT'S AFTER SOMETHING IN THE BANK AND CREDIT UNION AT 23RD AND PROSPECT.

I KNOW IT.

AND WE'RE GOOD TO GO. ANYTIME, BATMAN.

NO TIME LIKE THE PRESENT.

THAT'S A GO. JUST REMEMBER... THINK BAT-THOUGHTS.

BAT-THOUGHTS. ONLY AND EVER.

CLICK

Bat-thoughts. **Bat**-thoughts. **Bat-thoughts**...all right, here we go.

First. You're not plummeting. You're swooping. **Swooping.**

Second, you did not leave the stove on.

Third, that doesn't even matter, because you are not Jim Gordon. Not today. Not anymore.

Right here, right now...

You...are...

You'll practice that.

Now, giant energy-man, what brings you to Little Cuba?!

I mean, sure, good people, good food. Best baseball player in Gotham history lives here. Dodger Valera. Five-ring catcher.

So what is it you're here t--

BOOOM

BATMAN, ARE YOU ALL RIGHT?!

⇒Unh⇐ Bat-thoughts... that hurt. A lot.

Damn, Jim...

I MEAN, THAT'S *WILLIAMS.* THE GUY IS QUICK AS A WHIP. TOP OF HIS CLASS...

YES. AND HE'D MAKE A MUCH *SMARTER* BATMAN THAN YOU, JIM.

RIGHT. OF COURSE HE WOULD. OR *HUANG.* LOOK AT HER. SHE PRACTICALLY *LIVES* AT THE STATION.

YES. AND SHE'D MAKE A MUCH *TOUGHER* BATMAN THAN YOU.

HELL, THEY'D ALL BE *PRETTIER* BATMEN THAN YOU, I'LL SAY THAT.

BUT NONE OF THEM WOULD BE THE *RIGHT* BATMAN.

YOU WERE A *MARINE,* COMMISSIONER. SO WAS I. THOSE KIDS, AND THEY *ARE* KIDS, THEY'LL GET *HURT* OUT THERE.

NOW THE OTHER BOARD MEMBERS, THEY'D PREFER A YOUNGER BATMAN. A MORE FRESH-FACED BATMAN. EVEN THOUGH THE PUBLIC WON'T KNOW BATMAN'S IDENTITY. BUT ME? I BELIEVE IT *HAS* TO BE YOU.

FORGIVE ME, GERI, BUT... WHY?

BECAUSE YOU KNOW THE *CITY* BETTER THAN ANYONE ELSE. YOU'LL MAKE AN UGLY BATMAN, SURE. BUT YOU'LL MAKE THE *BEST* BATMAN. ONE THAT'LL LET ME SLEEP AT NIGHT, KNOWING THIS BATTERED, BEATEN CITY...IS SAFE.

LOOK, I KNOW THE IDEA IS SCARY. BATMAN IS THIS...TERRIFYING, GIANT THING. BUT IT'S JUST AN *ILLUSION.* HE WAS A *MAN,* JIM. THE RIGHT MAN AT THE TIME.

BUT YOU'RE THE RIGHT MAN *NOW.* I'M TELLING YOU. WHAT DO YOU SAY?

... I'M SORRY...

NOT FEELING TOO *STEALTHY* TONIGHT, BATS?

OH, SORRY, I WAS JUST SHOWING THIS STUFF OFF.

I DIDN'T KNOW YOU PARTOOK OF CANCER CANDY, *WILLIAMS.*

I DON'T, LIEUTENANT BULLOCK. I WAS JUST COMING UP HERE TO FACE-CHAT WITH MY KID. ELEVEN MONTHS TODAY.

WON'T SLEEP FOR CRAP, BUT HEY, HE'S BLOOD.

CUTE. GO ON. DON'T MIND US.

GIMME THAT.

YOU KNOW YOU'RE GOING TO HAVE TO GET *LASIK*, RIGHT?

"THE EYES. HOW DO I WORK THEM?!"

ON IT. WHAT ARE WE LOOKING FOR?

UNH! SOMEONE STEALING HOME!

I DON'T UNDERSTAND, IF--

THE MONSTER IS AN EXTENSION OF A PARTICULAR CRIMINAL. AND WHAT DO WE KNOW ABOUT THEM?

THEY WERE ATTACKING A BANK.

BUT MOST OF THE CASH IN THAT BANK IS TRACEABLE. SO WHAT'RE THEY REALLY AFTER?

THE MOST VALUABLE STASH IN LITTLE CUBA...

...BELONGS TO ITS MOST FAMOUS RESIDENT...

DODGER VALERA.

Huh. LOOK AT THAT. BATMAN SWINGS AND CONNECTS!

PRECIOUS PRECIOUS. YES, HIS REAL NAME. I KNOW HIM WELL. FOUNDING MEMBER OF THE CUBAN BRANCH OF THE INFAMOUS WHISPER GANG.

STRANGE, THE POWER SOURCE SEEMS TO BE COMING FROM INSIDE THE PERP. WE HAVE IDENTIFICATION, THOUGH. HIS NAME IS--

UPON INITIATION, THE GANG MAKES ITS MEMBERS WEAR METAL MASKS FOR A YEAR TO PROVE THEIR DEDICATION. PRECIOUS OPTED TO KEEP HIS ON FOR THREE. HENCE THE SCARS. MURDER, EXTORTION...

"I THINK SO."

"GOOD. THEN LISTEN CAREFULLY, BECAUSE THIS IS THE MOST *IMPORTANT* PART...

"WHAT WE'RE MAKING HERE IS SOMETHING DANGEROUS AND UNKNOWN.

"YOU WILL BE A NEW BATMAN, IF YOU DO THIS, JIM.

"YOU WON'T *BE* POLICE, YOU'LL WORK WITH THEM. WITH THE LOCAL GOVERNMENTS, AND THE PEOPLE, TOO. YOU'LL BE A BATMAN THAT HAS CHECKS AND BALANCES.

"YOU'LL BE A *BETTER* BATMAN, BETTER FOR THIS GOTHAM, THIS MOMENT.

"SOMETHING INSPIRING."

"NOW, THE PUBLIC WON'T KNOW YOUR IDENTITY, BUT THE FEW THAT *NEED* TO KNOW, WILL.

"YOU'LL HAVE TO TRAIN, TO *TRANSFORM* YOURSELF.

"AND YOU'LL LIVE IN AN APARTMENT IN OUR MAIN FACILITY. IT'LL BE YOUR HOME. YOUR 'CAVE.'

"SO, JIM GORDON...WHAT DO YOU SAY?"

Heh.

I GUESS THEY'LL HAVE TO START MAKING THESE DAMN THINGS

— HARV

"I SAY..."

WHAT THE HELL HAVE WE DONE?

...BRUCE WAYNE?

CUTE. BUT I *WASN'T* ASKING ABOUT THE SMOKING. I WAS ASKING WHETHER YOU'RE ALL RIGHT WITH WHAT YOU FOUND OUT. AT THE *MORGUE.*

...

AW. ARE THOSE LITTLE HORNS? YOU ROCKSTAR.

BARBARA DREW THEM ON, FOR INSPIRATION.

I'M FINE.

THUNK

OKAY THEN.

HEY, *DARYL?!* DO ME A FAVOR? TURN ON THE LIGHTS DOWN HERE AND SHOW JIM HIS BATMOBILE.

SURE THING...

KLIK

I'VE GOTTEN HUNDREDS OF PINGS IN JUST THE LAST MINUTE. THE *BAT-APP* IS GOING CRAZY. IT'S ANOTHER MASSIVE DISTURBANCE IN THE *NARROWS*. CHINATOWN THIS TIME.

"BAT APP." TRANSLATE TO OLD PERSON FOR ME.

DARYL DEVELOPED A BATMAN APP IN THE DAYS AFTER BATMAN DIED. IF YOU HAVE IT ON YOUR PHONE, AND YOU'RE IN TROUBLE, IT LETS ANYONE IN A TWO HUNDRED FOOT RADIUS KNOW THAT YOU NEED HELP.

IT'S SO WE CAN WATCH OUT FOR EACH OTHER. *THAT'S* BATMAN.

TO ME AT LEAST.

AND...IT HAS A BARB THAT FUNNELS ALL *ALERTS* TO US, UP HERE. SO WE GET A BOOTS-ON-THE-GROUND JUMP ON ANY CRIME. BEFORE THE NINE-ONE-ONE CALLS, EVEN.

HEH. SEE, *THAT'S* BATMAN. TO ME AT LEAST.

JUMPING?

BAT-STACHE AWAY.

Look at that.

It'll never stop being strange, will it? Seeing the city from above. Seeing the whole.

Before this, every day, every moment, your job was about seeing it from the street.

And the city is **hurting** right now. You can see the gashes. Deep ones, left by the Joker.

Especially here. In the **Narrows**.

It's Gotham's poorest neighborhood. Made up of nearly a dozen diverse communities. It's been let down over and over by the mechanisms put in place to protect it.

Under-protected. Under-represented. It's been burned so many times, you can practically feel the embers everywhere.

Without help from the city, it establishes its own forms of protection and justice. From community groups to gangs. All **independent**.

Like the old Batman.

And here you are, an extension of the very **system** that's failed them so many times, but a system you've believed in and fought for your whole life...here you are, coming along, telling them to believe in you.

You're going to have to prove yourself to them, Batman. You're going to have to rebuild all that lost **trust**. Brick by--

THANKS FOR THE HELP, COMMISSIONER. KEEP ME POSTED IF ANYTHING ELSE COMES UP.

I'M AFRAID I CAN'T DO THAT.

WHAT?

LOOK, I KNOW IN GOTHAM THERE'S ALWAYS BEEN A BATMAN STANDING WITH A COMMISSIONER ON A ROOFTOP SOMEWHERE, TALKING IN SECRET, BUT NOT AFTER TODAY.

*POWERS CORP* AND THE CITY WANT GCPD TAKING LEAD ON THIS, JIM. WHEN WE'RE READY TO MOVE IN ON HIM, WE'LL CALL YOU. YOU CAN COLLAR HIM AND TAKE A BOW.

BUT, MAGGIE...

LISTEN TO ME. YOU'RE BATMAN. BUT A *DEPUTIZED* BATMAN. STATE MONEY. STATE BOSSES. YOU'RE OFFICIAL. AND "OFFICIAL" MEANS RULES. YOU DON'T FOLLOW THOSE RULES, THEY'LL SHUT YOU DOWN HARD. THAT I KNOW.

AND IF I DO?

⇒*Sigh*⇐ I DON'T KNOW, JIM. BATMAN'S ALWAYS BEEN ON THE OTHER SIDE OF THE FENCE FOR ME. AND HERE YOU ARE...IF YOU'RE ASKING ME IF I THINK IT COULD WORK? HONESTLY, I'D SAY GET OUT NOW.

THAT'S WHAT YOU CAME HERE TO TELL ME, ISN'T IT?

NO ONE WOULD THINK LESS OF YOU.

I HAVE TO GO.

ALL RIGHT. WELL, AT LEAST I KNOW YOU WON'T DISAPPEAR ON ME, RIGHT?

...

DIGITAL CAMOUFLAGE.

TOUCHE. WELL, FOR WHAT IT'S WORTH...

UNH!

BATMAN YOU HAVE TO EJECT! *NOW!*

SHE'S RIGHT! THE SUIT...

...IT CAN'T TAKE MUCH MORE! IT'S GOING TO IMPLODE.

BLOODY HELL, GET OUT OF THERE, BATMAN!

I'M TRYING, *DAMMIT!*

Try all you want, idiot. But this is where the road takes you, literally.

Sawyer was right. They were all right. You were a damn fool. Over before you started. You're not Batman. You don't even have a--

OH. WAIT...

BUT... BUT...

BREATHE, DARYL. JUST BREATHE.

...BAT-TRUCK...

GEE, WE NEED TO GET YOU TO A HOSPITAL NOW. THAT "SEED" IN YOUR ANKLE. WHOEVER GAVE IT TO YOU--

WILL COME FOR YOU, OFFICER BATMAN.

HE'S GROWING A WHOLE GARDEN OF US...*MR. BLOOM*...

MR. BLOOM? WHO IS THAT?

⇥Gasp!⇤

GEE! GEE! WHO?!

FACT IS... I DON'T KNOW *WHAT* THE HELL TO THINK ANYMORE.

HEY, YOU. I DIDN'T SEE YOU COME IN THIS MORNING.

I GOT HERE EARLY. THE AIR CONDITIONING NEEDED WORK.

AREN'T YOU THE MORNING PERSON. CAN YOU GRAB SOME CLAY FROM THE STORE-ROOM? BLOCKS, NOT BAGS.

BLOCKS NOT BAGS, SAYS BOSS JULIE MADISON.

HELLO, BRUCE.

WHO ARE YOU, AND WHAT ARE YOU DOING IN--

...

IT'S SIMPLE.

I'M BATMAN.

AND WE NEED TO TALK...

HERE, THIS ONE'S BEEN NEUTRALIZED.

I STILL DON'T UNDERSTAND WHY YOU'RE TELLING *ME* THIS.

BECAUSE...

...BECAUSE YOU'RE THE *KEY* TO BATMAN, BRUCE.

AT LEAST, FOR *ME* YOU ARE.

YOU SEE, THE SUIT I WEAR, *YOU* DEVELOPED MOST OF THE TECH IN IT. WHEN POWERS ABSORBED WAYNE INDUSTRIES, THEY CO-OPTED IT, BUT IT'S STILL *YOUR* TECH.

AND I WAS HOPING YOU MIGHT HELP ME...RECONFIGURE SOME OF THE PROGRAMMING SO THAT I MIGHT BE ABLE TO DO SOME WORK AS BATMAN, BUT *PRIVATELY*.

EVERYTHING I DO, EVERYTHING I SEE, IT'S TRACKED BY POWERS AND PROCESSED BY THE POLICE. I'M JUST A MIDDLEMAN. A *SENTINEL*. BUT BATMAN...HE NEEDS TO BE SOMETHING *MORE*.

LOOK, SOMETHING BIG IS COMING TO GOTHAM. THIS MR. BLOOM, I HAVE A HUNCH ABOUT HIM. IT INVOLVES SOMETHING THAT HAPPENED YEARS AGO. WILL YOU HELP ME?

IT'S FUNNY, MR. GORDON. THIS REC CENTER? IT WAS SET UP BY LUCIUS FOX, A FRIEND OF MY FATHER'S. HE BUILT IT FOR ALL THE NEIGHBORHOODS OF THE NARROWS. THE CORNER. LITTLE CUBA...A SAFE PLACE FOR KIDS TO COME, TO PLAY. TO *TALK*.

WHEN LUCIUS OPENED THE DOORS, HE STARTED A POLICY. ON YOUR FIRST DAY HERE, YOU HAVE TO MAKE A *BRICK*. YOU CUT THE CLAY, YOU PAINT IT, YOU PUT IT IN THE KILN. BAKE IT. THEN YOU PUT IT OUT BACK. THERE'S A *WALL*. SOME BRICKS ARE FROM DECADES AGO.

NOW, WITH THE WAY THIS NEIGHBORHOOD WAS WRECKED DURING THE JOKER'S ATTACK, A LOT OF THE KIDS ARE MISSING HOMES, FRIENDS, *FAMILY* MEMBERS...

BUT THEIR BRICKS ARE HERE WHEN THEY COME. THEY'RE ALWAYS OUT BACK, IN THE WALL.

BRUCE--

NO, LISTEN TO ME. WHOEVER I WAS BEFORE...I'M NOT THAT PERSON ANYMORE. I *CAN'T* BE. AND THESE KIDS, HERE AT THE CENTER, I CARE ABOUT THEM. I CARE ABOUT THIS. I'M TRYING TO BUILD A LIFE. USING THE MOST BASIC BLOCKS. DO YOU UNDERSTAND ME?

BRUCE, I WASN'T TRYING TO--

BRUCE?

EVERYTHING ALL RIGHT?

EVERYTHING'S FINE, MISS MADISON.

COMMISSIONER GORDON? PLEASE, STAY FOR LUNCH. AND CALL ME *JULIE.* I ALMOST DIDN'T RECOGNIZE YOU WITHOUT YOUR MUSTACHE. AND WITH...MUSCLES.

IMPLANTS. EVERYWHERE IMPLANTS. AND THANKS, BUT I SHOULD BE GOING.

YOU CAN KEEP THAT. GOOD SEEING YOU, BRUCE.

YOU OKAY, HON? WHAT DID HE WANT?

NOTHING. HE JUST...HAD THE *WRONG* GUY.

"THAT'S NOT *BRUCE WAYNE.*"

BUT IT'S *NOT* BRUCE. I'M LOOKING AT THIS MIND, RIGHT NOW, AND IT'S NOT *BRUCE WAYNE'S* MIND. IT IS, IN *SOME* WAYS...BUT IN OTHERS...

...IN OTHERS IT'S NOT. SO WHAT HAPPENED TO HIM?

WHAT HAPPENED IS THAT HE DIED. AFTER HIS FIGHT WITH THE JOKER, HE WAS DEAD FOR HOURS. HIS HEART STOPPED. HIS BRAIN DIED.

BUT THEN HE WAS... *HEALED.*

...

THE *DIONESIUM.* OF COURSE. THE PATHWAYS OF HIS BRAIN ARE ENTIRELY DIFFERENT. IT MUST HAVE SEEPED INTO HIS BROKEN SKULL, HEALED THE DEAD TISSUE, BUT IN DOING SO, IT...

IT BROUGHT HIM BACK *NEW.* HE WAS BRUCE, BUT WITH NO HISTORY. NO...*SHADOW* WATCHING.

BUT YOU *TOLD* HIM, ALFRED. YOU TOLD HIM ABOUT HIS LIFE.

I DID. IT WAS ONE OF THE WORST THINGS I'VE EVER HAD TO DO.

"TO WALK THIS MAN THROUGH THE *TRAGEDY* OF HIS OWN LIFE AGAIN. TO TAKE HIM, UNFORMED, THIS PERSON YOU LOVE, AND TWIST THE *CLAY* OF THEM INTO A MALFORMED THING. WORKING MY WAY TO *BATMAN.*

"I TOLD HIM HE'D BEEN IN AN ACCIDENT DURING THE JOKER'S ATTACK, AND THEN I STARTED AT THE BEGINNING. I TOLD HIM ABOUT HIS CHILDHOOD, ABOUT HIS *PARENTS' DEATH.* I TOLD HIM HOW WHEN THEY DIED, HE'D BECOME ANGRY, DRIVEN... HOW HE'D TURNED THAT INTO FUEL TO *HELP* THE CITY.

"HOW HE'D BUILT WAYNE ENTERPRISES INTO SOMETHING *HEROIC* AND SPECIAL.

"HOW HE'D BEEN A *SYMBOL.* ALL THE WHILE, WORKING MY WAY TO THE LAST TRUTH. A TERRIBLE MONOLOGUE ON A TERRIBLE STAGE."

"AND I WAS JUST ABOUT TO TELL HIM THE LAST TRUTH, TO OPEN THAT LAST, WORST DOOR, WHEN--"

STOP.

I'VE HEARD ENOUGH, ALFRED.

BUT THERE'S MORE, BRUCE.

I'M SURE THERE IS.

I DON'T KNOW WHAT THIS ACCIDENT DID TO ME, BUT I'M... I'M NOT THE PERSON YOU'RE DESCRIBING. I KNOW WHAT YOU'RE SAYING IS TRUE. I KNOW I LOVED YOU. I LOOK AT THESE PICTURES, AND I KNOW I LOVED *THEM.* BUT I DON'T FEEL THEIR LOSS.

I FEEL TERRIBLE FOR THAT BOY IN THE ALLEY, BUT I CAN'T BE WHO HE WAS. IT'S NOT WHO I AM.

...

WELL, THEN...WHO ON EARTH ARE YOU, MASTER BRUCE?

"FOR TWO DAYS, I DIDN'T SEE HIM.

"AND THEN, ON THE THIRD DAY, HE REAPPEARED AND SAID SOMETHING THAT LIFTED MY HEART."

I MAY NOT BE THE MAN I WAS, BUT I WANT TO HELP. IN MY OWN WAY, THOUGH. FACE-TO-FACE. MY MOTHER WORKED IN SCHOOLS. MY FATHER WORKED IN CITY HOSPITALS. THAT FEELS RIGHT. THAT FEELS LIKE ME.

"NOW THIS CITY, MR. KENT, IT NEVER GIVES ANYTHING BACK. *NEVER.*

"BUT I SWEAR TO YOU, NOT A MINUTE AFTER BRUCE SAID THIS TO ME, THE DOORBELL RANG.

"A *MISS JULIE MADISON,* COMING TO CHECK ON BRUCE. SHE'D HEARD HE'D HAD AN ACCIDENT DURING THE ATTACK. A GIRLFRIEND FROM HIS YOUTH. WORKING WITH CHILDREN IN THE NARROWS...

"THE CITY...IT NEVER GIVES. BUT IT GAVE."

YOU HAVE TO TELL HIM, ALFRED. NOT JUST THAT HE'S BRUCE WAYNE, BUT THAT HE'S *BATMAN.*

I'M SORRY, BUT IF YOU DON'T, *I* WILL.

IS THAT SO?

ALFRED... WHAT ARE YOU...?!

GO AHEAD, FLY TO HIM. TELL HIM. BUT BEFORE YOU DO, KNOW THIS.

BRUCE WAYNE HAS NO COMBAT SKILLS. NO *DETECTION* SKILLS. EVERY BIT OF HIS FIFTEEN YEARS OF *TRAINING* AND EXPERIENCE AS BATMAN IS GONE.

AND IT'S NOT RECOVERABLE, BECAUSE THE MEMORIES WERE *NEVER THERE.* IT'S A NEW BRAIN.

ASKING HIM TO BE BATMAN IS LIKE ME TELLING YOU TO *FLY* UNDER THIS RING'S GLOW. HE IS *POWERLESS,* AND TO WEAR THE COWL WOULD BE A DEATH SENTENCE.

YOU'RE THINKING HE CAN RE-LEARN IT. MAYBE HE CAN, OVER YEARS. BUT REMEMBER THE MOST IMPORTANT THING...

...BATMAN WAS BORN FROM THE SCREAMS OF A YOUNG BOY IN AN ALLEY. FROM HIS PRIMAL PAIN AND ANGER. FROM A SCAR. BUT THAT *SCAR* IS GONE, MR. KENT. HEALED.

ALFRED, YOU CAN SHOW ME IMAGES OF HIS BRAIN, BUT HE'S *BATMAN.* HE'S ALWAYS GOT A WAY OUT. A WAY BACK.

FOLLOW ME A MOMENT, MR. KENT. I DIDN'T BRING YOU HERE TO SHOW YOU IMAGES OF BRUCE'S BRAIN.

I BROUGHT YOU HERE TO SHOW YOU *THIS.*

WHAT IS IT?

SOMETHING HE HID. FROM ALL OF US. BATMAN'S *FINAL INVENTION.*

IT'S A MACHINE MEANT TO ENSURE THAT THERE WOULD ALWAYS BE A *BATMAN*. A MACHINE THAT HE WAS WORKING ON IN SECRET WHEN HE DIED.

IT WOULD USE HIS DNA TO GROW EACH SUCCESSIVE BRUCE TO AGE TWENTY-SEVEN, INSTILL IN HIM ALL THE ORIGINAL *BRUCE'S* PAIN, ALL HIS TRAINING, ALL HIS MEMORIES, UP TO THE MOMENT HE DECIDED TO BECOME *BATMAN*.

...

IS THIS...?

PICTURE IT...

...PICTURE AN ENDLESS CHAIN OF TRAGEDY. EACH VERSION OF HIM SUBJECTED TO THE SAME *HORRORS*.

BRUCE KILLED BY BATMAN SO THAT HE, BATMAN, COULD BE BORN AGAIN. AN *UNNATURAL* GENEOLOGY OF THEM.

"YES, FATHER, I SHALL BECOME A BAT," BUT SPOKEN BY BRUCE TO BATMAN, FATHERED BY BATMAN. ONE REPLACING THE NEXT, GENERATION TO GENERATION.

BUT EVEN HE, WITH ALL HIS GENIUS, HE NEVER EVEN CAME CLOSE TO FINISHING IT.

->Huff<-
->huff<- I *HATE*
ROBOCOP.

*BATMAN!*

CLIK

OKAY, I'M
RUNNING A
TRACE ON--

WAIT,
HANG ON.
SOMETHING'S--
BATMAN, QI'S
STILL UP!
HE'S--

WSH

ARE YOU
ALL RIGHT? THE
READINGS ON
THE ROOM...

->Ungh<- I'M FINE.
IT'S AN INDUSTRIAL
*FURNACE.* FOR DESTROYING
EVIDENCE. STEEL WALLS,
LEAD-BACKED. NO WAY OUT.

GOOD
GOD, THE
TEMPERATURE...

I'M
COMING IN,
I'M GOING
TO--

->Ungh!<-

*TWO
HUNDRED* AND
->Ungh<- ...RISING.
*FAST.* NO
EXIT.

BATMAN,
THE SUIT CAN'T
WITHSTAND THAT!
YOU'RE GOING TO
BE COOKED ALIVE!

->Huff huff<-
JULIA! JULIA,
COME IN!

"COME IN

...EARTH TO BRUCE!

*Huh!*

YOU OKAY?

I'M SORRY. I WAS JUST LOOKING OVER *DUKE THOMAS'* FILE. HE STILL...→YAWN←. HE STILL HAS IT *IN* FOR ME.

WELL, YOU DO HAVE HISTORY WITH HIM. I KNOW NOT *YOU*-YOU, BUT STILL. I'M SURE IT'S WEIRD FOR HIM. AND YOU.

IT'S ODD. I FEEL LIKE I HAVEN'T SLEPT IN YEARS. AND THEN WAKING UP, IT STILL ALL FEELS...

NEW?

IT'S OKAY. COME ON, LET'S GO HOME.

LUCIUS FOX C...

"THAT ONE'S NOT FOR YOU..."

THIS ONE. THIS ONE IS YOURS.

IF YOU SEWED IT IN, IT'D COME TO LIFE.

WHAT DO YOU THINK?

I THINK...

I NEVER NEEDED POWERS TO *WIELD* POWER HERE IN GOTHAM, *"MR. BLOOM,"* AND I'M NOT SURE I NEED THEM NOW. BUT...PEOPLE SEEM TO BE BUYING WHAT YOU'RE SELLING. SO I'M INTERESTED.

BUT I'M SO SORRY, MR. COBBLEPOT. I THINK WE'VE MISUNDERSTOOD EACH OTHER. THAT SEED *WOULD* WORK FOR YOU, FOR YOUR BODY, BUT I CAN'T GIVE IT TO YOU.

*Heh.* IS THAT SO? AND WHY NOT? YOU DON'T HAVE ENOUGH?

NO, I DO. I HAVE TOO MANY. IT'S JUST...YOU'RE NOT PART OF THIS.

*Ah.*

WELL, I DO FIND THIS ALL VERY CUTE, MR. BLOOM. I'VE BEEN HEARING ABOUT YOU FOR A BIT. THE MAN WHO GIVES AWAY POWERS. A WEAPONS DEALER WHO MAKES NO DEALS. GROWING SOMETHING. A *GARDEN.* A BUSINESS.

GOTHAM MARSHES. POST-ZERO YEAR.

The body lies less than one foot from the old city limit.

A boy, not even sixteen years old. A kid.

A kid left for the crows.

SEE HIS I.D.

"YOU'RE *UPGRADING*.

"YOU SAID HE'S FROM THE CORNER. THE *FOUR FIVES* HAVE BEEN AGGRESSIVE THERE LATELY. FEUDING WITH THE BIRD. COULD BE THEM."

I'D AGREE, IF THE *SHOTS* HAD KILLED HIM.

BUT I SCANNED HIM. HE DIED FROM A *FALL*. DROPPED HERE. FROM ABOUT A THOUSAND FEET UP.

...

KANE MUNICIPAL AIRPORT IS ON THE OTHER SIDE OF TOWN, AND ALL POLICE BLIMPS WERE DECOMMISSIONED WEEKS AGO. IT'S RAINCLOUDS AND GEESE.

NO ONE FLIES OVER THIS AREA.

SOMEONE DID.

ALL RIGHT. I'LL TRACK THE SHOTS. YOU HAVE LEADS?

BATMAN?

In the past few months, since he defeated the so-called *Riddler*, more and more enemies have risen. The city has barely recovered, and in some places, it hasn't recovered at all. Crime is at a peak. And now these "super-villains..."

Each has a vendetta with the city. And with each of them, he has tried to draw their fire, to become the target. Every day a new one. Every day the city in peril. He's almost used to it. A year in and it's a tale he knows by heart, one that ends with him.

MR. FREEZE

POISON IV

PENGUIN

KILLER CROC

CLAYFACE

Now, in his mind, he moves through the gallery of these enemies, until he lands on the one with a connection to the Corner. And things airborne...

**STOP IT! STOP IT, WHAT ARE YOU DOING, YOU LUNATIC?!**

Batman tells Cobblepot that he's become predictable. So much so that after the last time they fought, Batman put a grounder in his suit. 'Give the power back.' Exactly."

Then he says the boy's name: Peter Duggio.

**PETER WHO-GIO?!! I HAVE NO IDEA WHAT YOU'RE TALKING ABOUT! WHY CAN'T YOU JUST LEAVE ME ALONE AND GO AFTER GOTHAM'S *REAL* CRIMINALS?!!**

If COBBLEPOT means the Gotham politicos who turn a blind eye while he lines their pockets, Batman knows all about them. He's read up.

But the Gazette has uncovered substantial links between well known, legitimate lobbyists and Gotham's own underworld. During a year-long investigation, the Gazette found that at least three prominent advocacy groups regularly accepted donations from active criminal organizations looking to influence the city legislature.

One source, speaking anonymously, explained,

"Regulation who profits from where a line sits. It moves according to who pays for it to move. The real criminals are the men and women who paint the line."

But today is not about them.

**TODAY, I'M GOING AFTER YOU.**

SERUM BIRD FEED

Batman knows all he has to do...is wait.

Until the story comes.

And the story begins with coils. Coils upon coils.

NOT A CHANCE. WE'RE GOING TO NEED AT LEAST A MILE MORE. LOOPED, WITH *TRIPLE* THE SURFACE AREA.

WE'RE TALKING ABOUT FREEZING A GOOD QUARTER MILE OF THE GOTHAM RIVER, AND THAT'S JUST THE *DAMN* GROUND FLOOR.

MR. COBBLEPOT?

WHAT THE HELL DO YOU WANT FROM ME,...?

PETER.

PETER DUGGIO.

I WANT TO DO BUSINESS.

HEH. AND WHAT DO YOU KNOW ABOUT BUSINESS, KID?

I KNOW I HAVE SOMETHING TO OFFER, AND YOU HAVE SOMETHING I WANT. SO WE SHOULD DO BUSINESS.

GROCERY

#373 GOTHAM DELI GROCERY

SANDWICH COFFEE

Turned out Peter was running a bodega. It wasn't much, but nothing in the Corner was. Still, it was one of the only businesses owned by a man who lived there in the 'hood. Peter's father.

Admittedly, Cobblepot was amused by him. So he gave the boy thirty seconds to explain.

But now, after the Zero Year attack, Peter's father was down. And unlikely to recover, and the bank, suddenly looking to invest in the rebuilding of the area, wanted the bodega and the building that housed it.

There was a game Bruce used to play as a boy. He'd heard anecdotes about how the Miagani Indians put their fingers to the ground to "listen" for coming changes in the land.

Bruce would put his finger to the tracks by his house. "Listening" for some message from Gotham City, trying to hear all it had to tell him.

What Cobblepot said, it stays with him.

He's been away for over a decade, training, but he knows this city. He grew up here, his family has been here for generations. And he's done his research.

This place, the Corner. Predominantly African-American for over a century. Little opportunity. Little protection...

reached a peak of 1963 during demonstrations protesting segregation policies by multiple Gotham ies similar to other suburban areas like Levittown, NY, which barred blacks from renting homes. Protestors and community groups claimed policies were essentially "constructing a slum" out of T... Corner by restricting mo... for working and middle... residents. The protes... robust, and Goth...

employed fire hoses, dogs and what was called "measured violence" to end the demonstrations.

...he knows the history. But above all, he knows what matters is stopping who killed Peter.

The Corner store... torched. The sight makes him more determined.

Outside, kids mull about. They look at him like they want to talk. But not about the case. About their lives, about everyday concerns.

He scares them home. Away from all of this, hopefully.

So the boy, Peter, went to the Penguin for help, to keep the store away from the Four Fives...

And the Penguin took it, and turned around and gifted it to the gang, a peace offering.

Leaving the boy with nothing. Nothing but a target on his back.

"NEVER SAW THE LITTLE BROTHA LIKE THAT, ALL AMPED'N...

"RAGE.

"WOULD HAVE, MIGHT A OFFERED HIM A SPOT IN THE CREW...

"KID WAS ON *FIRE.*"

THEN IT WAS OVER. I'M NOT THE BAD GUY HERE--I'M JUST *HERE.*

*It's all there in his sneer. Between his teeth.*

...still, the Four Fives, originally the Green Line Fours, founded in 1971 in Gotham's Corner district ...named for 4th street and 5th avenue, the intersection at the edge of the neigh-

*Between the lines.*

nia ...people today would be surprised to know the Four Fives originated as a neighborhood radicalized watch group. With the Corner les...

*Some line of defense that Batman already knows.*

nearly every other neighborhood, the four...

also provided ... wasn't until the 1980's and the infusion of cheap, hard drugs that the group became known as a ...et gang." In fact, the

*None of it matters in this burned-out place. And he's about to tell Tano so, when the **call** comes.*

WHAT DID YOU FIND?

BAD THINGS. FOR ONE, THE KID, PETER, HE WENT TO THE GANG UNIT FOR HELP.

AND?

AND THEY BLEW HIM OFF.

AND?

AND I GOT A NAME ON THE BULLETS. NOTHING GOOD.

Too much for today especially, because here,
now, Batman is just out to get the story, to
catch the one who put Peter down.

And Howler is still talking to him,
about guns, about the firepower
on the streets these days. About
a lack of training. About no
acclimation to the neighborhood.

And Batman
knows all this.

But it's not
what he's after.

"...I TOLD HIM TO GO TO *BRUCE WAYNE*."

MR. WAYNE! BRUCE WAYNE! HEY!

"PETER'S STORE WAS ONLY WORTH SOMETHING ONCE BRUCE WAYNE ANNOUNCED HE WAS GONNA DEVELOP THE NEIGHBORHOOD. I SAID TO PETER, I SAID, 'YOU SHOULD TRY TALKING TO THE MAN.' ASKING HIM TO HELP, OR NOT TO BUILD. I DON'T KNOW...

While some think an infusion of capital is needed, others question whether private developments -- even ones like Wayne Apartments, designed to provide upscale living conditions for lower-middle class families in the Corner -- might drive up property values and force out longtime residents. The debat~~e~~ ~~has p~~roponents on both sides, but in

"BUT IT DIDN'T WORK.

"AND THAT WAS IT. NO MORE OPTIONS. THAT'S WHEN HE STARTED TALKING ABOUT *IT*."

ABOUT WHAT?

ABOUT YOU. HE WANTED TO STAND UP FOR HIMSELF. TO PUSH BACK.

LIKE *YOU* DO.

...

HOW?

THERE'S A PLACE, BATMAN...

And now the story takes a turn toward an alley at the edge of the Corner. No name now, but long ago it was called *Blossom Row*.

Batman knows its history.

And now he learns its present... It cuts through a part of the Corner no one has bothered to clean up since Zero Year.

It's overgrown and wild.

A place you go when you've had it with things, such as they are.

A special place. A garden. Where new things can be grown.

The report comes back from Jim, and it's as Batman suspected.

In Peter's blood, a substance, culled from the work of Dr. Kirk Langstrom, and bonded with steroidal venom and other components. A back-alley mixture. Sophisticated and raw, all at once.

It would have given him strength and speed...and with a trigger, some catastrophic damage, it could have even mutated, changed him.

The man who gave Peter the stuff is long gone, no trace.

But the mixture he gave Peter, it made him...into something more than he was, for a little while at least, until it wore off.

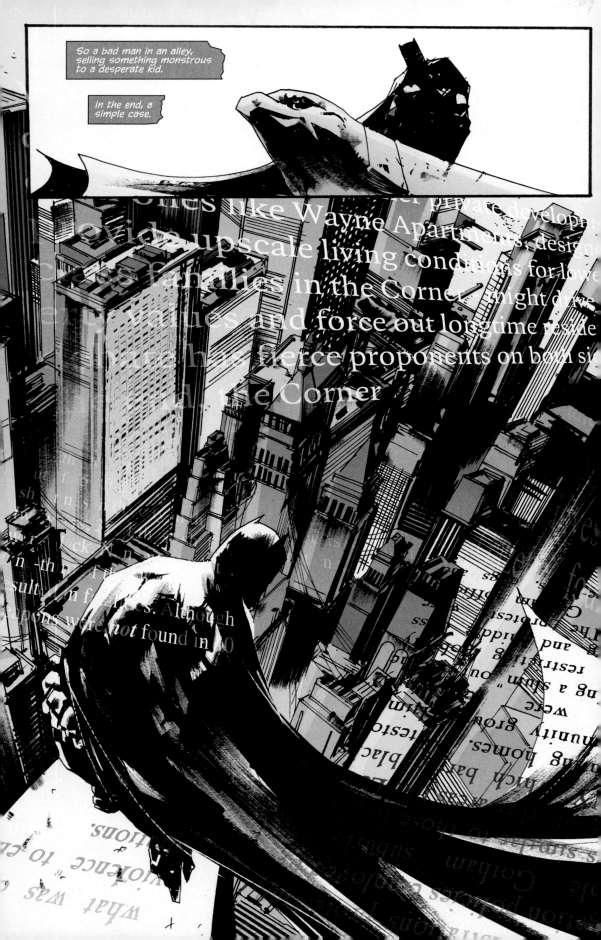

So a bad man in an alley, selling something monstrous to a desperate kid.

In the end, a simple case.

...people today would be surprised to know the Four Fives originated as a neighborhood radicalized watch group. With the Corner less policed than nearly every other neighbor... group." In... gang." In... Gotham's named district... 4th street and 5th avenue, the intersection...

provide upscale living conditions for lower-middle class families in the Corner - might drive up property values and force out longtime residents. The debate has fierce proponents on both sides, but in the end, the Corner

"THE PROBLEM WITH AUTHORITY" Continued

...the NAACP reported that out of 45 officer-involved shootings in the city in the last two years, 37 of those shot were black. None were white. ...third of the shootings ...led in fatalities. Although ...s were *not* found in 40

percent of cases, the NAACP found, no officers were charged, not one

"Regulation is about where a line sits. It essentially accepted donations active criminal profits from robust, and the protests were for working and middle class residents. The Gotham officers employed fire-hoses, dogs and "Constructing a slum," out of The Corner by restricting mobility policies claimed and community groups Protestors from removing homes barred blacks... suburban areas like Levit... which in N.Y... that... organizations looking to influence the city legislature... move. The real criminals are the men and nals are the men and who pays for it

The boy flew.

But Batman will stay.

Because he got it wrong.

He sees that now.

Because there was someone to catch.

Cobblepot.

Tano.

Howler.

The man in the alley.

Bruce Wayne.

The whole city. Everyone and no one.

But above all, the one to catch was the boy.

Before he fell.

He will do it next time.
He will catch someone.

IT'S HIM AGAIN! RUN!

WAIT. TALK TO ME.

YOU SERIOUS?

REALLY?

"IN THE BEGINNING, THERE WAS NOTHING.

"AND THEN...

"...THERE WAS BATMAN.

"AND THIS WAS GOOD."

This is very, very bad.

So, Batman, you got yourself trapped in an industrial furnace.

Gun is cooked.

Temperature is eight hundred degrees and--

No, make that **nine** hundred degrees and rising.

In about thirty seconds, this hot-box will reach fourteen hundred degrees, cremation level, and your suit will give out and you will literally be burnt to dust.

Alright, Batman...

...time to do something amazing.

NO ONE, TECHNICALLY.

DIE, YOU OVERSIZED...

I HAVE IT ON WHAT'S CALLED A NIMBLE AUTO PROGRAM RIGHT NOW. IT'S NEW. I... I SET A TARGET AND THE SUIT CALCULATES A PLAN TO REACH THAT TARGET.

IT'S VERY BASIC, BUT THE SUIT WILL ACT ON ITS OWN...

...AND USES CONTEXTUAL MATERIAL...

...TO ACHIEVE ITS GOAL.

"...GIANTS WALK THE EARTH."

KICKING A MAN WHILE HE'S *DOWN?* THAT'S NOT THE BRUCE I KNOW.

EXPLAIN YOURSELF.

I ASKED ALFRED TO CALL SOME OLD FRIENDS OF THE FAMILY ABOUT HAVING THIS ALL *REMOVED,* BUT YOU WERE RIGHT, JULES, IT'S INTRACTABLE.

THE CITY HAS MANDATED ALL THE WRECKAGE FROM THE *JOKER'S* ATTACK STAY HERE IN THIS MAKESHIFT DUMP UNTIL THEY CAN FIGURE OUT WHAT TO DO WITH IT.

IT'S SWEET THAT YOU TRIED, BUT I COULD HAVE TOLD YOU THEY WOULDN'T BUDGE.

THE WHOLE CITY GOT HIT HARD BY "ENDGAME," BUT THE NARROWS, WHEN THAT VIRUS STARTED...THE *DENSITY* OF PEOPLE HERE, THE LACK OF POLICE AND MILITARY...MORE BUILDINGS WENT DOWN, MORE LIVES WERE LOST THAN ANYWHERE ELSE IN GOTHAM. IT'S ALWAYS THAT WAY WITH A BIG ATTACK.

AND WITH THE CLEANUP...THIS PLACE IS LAST IN LINE.

"I FOUND MIGUEL, OLIVIA, AND RADIK OUT HERE THIS MORNING.

"THEY WERE THROWING DIRT OVER THE FENCE."

WHAT ARE YOU DOING, 'LIV? YOU KNOW WE'RE SUPPOSED TO STAY AWAY FROM THE LOT.

WE WERE JUST TRYING TO *HIDE* THIS STUFF, BRUCE, SO NO ONE WILL COME FOR IT AND USE IT THE WAY JOKER DID. IF WE COVER IT UP, MAYBE THEY WON'T COME.

LUCIUS FOX WANTED THIS TO BE A *REFUGE* FOR THESE KIDS. BUT THEY'RE JUST WAITING FOR THE NEXT HORROR, JULES. NOW RUMORS OF THIS NEW GUY...THIS *BLOOM.* AND THESE REMINDERS...

THESE KIDS DON'T FEEL SAFE. NOT REALLY.

JIM GORDON'S VISIT IS STILL ON YOUR MIND, ISN'T IT?

LISTEN TO ME, BRUCE. YOU DON'T REMEMBER THIS, BUT WHEN WE WERE KIDS, I WAS ALWAYS CONCERNED THAT MY FATHER WOULD *BREAK* OUT, OR BE LET OUT, OR JUST...SHOW UP. HE WAS A *BAD* MAN, BRUCE. YOU DON'T WANT TO KNOW ABOUT HIM.

...

"I WAS ALWAYS TOUGHENING MYSELF UP. READYING FOR THAT DAY. BUT YOU...THE THING ABOUT YOU WAS, YOU'D BEEN THROUGH SOMETHING TRAUMATIC, AND INSTEAD OF MAKING YOURSELF FEEL SAFE, LIKE ME...

"...YOU CHANNELED WHATEVER FEAR YOU FELT INTO MAKING *OTHER PEOPLE* FEEL BRAVE. I LOVED YOU FOR THAT."

WHEN I SAW YOU ON TV, YEARS LATER, YOU WERE DOING THE SAME THING, BUT FOR A *WHOLE* CITY.

AND WHAT I'M SAYING IS, IF YOU NEED TO DO THAT AGAIN, TO DO THIS ON A BIGGER SCALE, I'D UNDERSTAND.

WHAT *GORDON* WANTED... LOOK, I DON'T KNOW ANYTHING ABOUT ROBOTICS OR CRIMINOLOGY OR *ANY* OF IT. I DON'T HAVE WAYNE ENTERPRISES. I DON'T HAVE THE *MONEY* OR POSITION. SO IF YOU'RE ASKING IF I WANT TO BE THE PERSON I WAS BEFORE...

I WENT BACK TO THE MANOR THE OTHER DAY. JUST TO...SEE, I GUESS. I LOOKED THROUGH MY OLD CLOSETS. I EVEN TRIED ON MY SUITS.

THE THING IS, THERE WAS NO TRACE OF A LIFE THERE. THAT BRUCE HAD NO PICTURES ANYWHERE. NOT OF FAMILY OR FRIENDS. NOT OF THE PEOPLE HE'D HELPED.

MY PARENTS' DEATHS...IT DID SOMETHING TO HIM.

IT'S LIKE, BEHIND THE MISSION, HE DIDN'T REALLY EXIST.

THIS, BEING PART OF THINGS. IT FEELS RIGHT. BUT THEN... LOOK AT *THIS.* ALL THE DAMN HORROR.

WE'LL FIGURE OUT THE STUFF BACK HERE. AND FOR WHAT IT'S WORTH, WHAT YOU'RE DOING, IT MATTERS TO THOSE KIDS. TO RADIK AND MIGUEL AND OLIVIA. IT MATTERS TO A LOT OF PEOPLE. INCLUDING ME.

LISTEN, I WANT YOU TO KNOW I L--

SHUT UP.

LET'S GO BACK IN. SINCE THERE'S *NOTHING* WE CAN DO ABOUT THIS STUFF TODAY...

"...WE CAN FIX THIS."

BRRET BRRET

FIRE? WHAT THE...

BREAKING AND ENTERING, ACTUALLY.

NO ONE DOWNSTAIRS WOULD EVEN CALL UP. SO I JUST ACTIVATED YOUR PERSONAL FIRE ESCAPE.

SINCE JOKER, EVERYONE'S READY TO BOLT. THE PSYCHOLOGY OF THE CITY RIGHT NOW. SKITTISH.

TELL ME AGAIN WHY YOU DIDN'T TAKE THAT CROWN GENIUS GRANT INSTEAD OF ME, DUKE?

I'M STUBBORN. OR AN IDIOT.

IDIOT SOUNDS RIGHT. PLEASE TELL ME THERE'S SOME NEWS ON YOUR FOLKS. I KEEP CALLING INTO THE MISSING PERSONS CENTERS THEY SET UP AFTER JOKER'S ATTACK, BUT THERE'S NOTHING.

NOTHING ON MY END YET EITHER. BUT THEY'RE OKAY. I FEEL IT.

WELL, WHERE ARE YOU STAYING? WHO ARE--

I'M FINE, DARYL. I'M NOT HERE FOR HELP. OR I AM, BUT NOT ABOUT THAT.

I'M HERE FOR HELP ABOUT *THIS*.

WHERE'D YOU GET THIS? NO ONE KNOWS ABOUT THESE.

IT DOESN'T MATTER. WHAT I'M ASKING IS THAT YOU TELL ME WHAT YOU FIND OUT ABOUT IT. AND ABOUT *BLOOM*.

DUKE. NO ONE WANTS TO CATCH THIS GUY MORE THAN ME. *PETER DUGGIO* WAS MY COUSIN. HELL, I'M THE ONE WHO TOLD THE OLD BATMAN ABOUT THAT ALLEY. BUT BLOOM VANISHED BEFORE BATMAN FOUND HIM. THAT ALLEY WAS RAZED.

AND FOR YEARS I LOOKED. I NEARLY GOT BURNED ALIVE BY DAMN BANGERS LOOKING. YOU *KNOW* THIS. I'VE TOLD THE NEW BATMAN EVERYTHING. HE'S ON IT.

ALL I'M ASKING IS YOU LET ME HELP, DARYL.

HERE.

I HAD AN EXTRA ONE.

YOU HAVE TO BE KIDDING ME.

DUKE, BATMAN DOESN'T NEED A ROBIN RIGHT NOW.

THAT'S FINE. ROBIN DOESN'T NEED A BATMAN EITHER. BATMAN IS ON THE GARGOYLE. ROBIN...ROBIN IS ON THE *STREET*. IT'S US, SOLVING OUR PROBLEMS TOGETHER. I KNOW YOU WORK FOR *HIM*, BUT YOU'RE US, TOO. YOU AND ME, WE CAME UP TOGETHER. WE'RE FAM--

MISTER GUTIERREZ? IS EVERYTHING OKAY?

KNOCK KNOCK

DARYL.

⇥Sigh⇤ ALRIGHT, ALRIGHT...

"...I'LL SEE WHAT I CAN DO."

STAFF ONLY

STAFF ONLY

STAFF ONLY

BRUCE, WHAT'RE YOU--

THESE THINGS. THEY'RE NOT UGLY REMINDERS. THEY'RE *TROPHIES.* TESTAMENTS TO WHAT THE KIDS LIVED THROUGH. THEY SHOULD LOOK AT THEM AND FEEL *PROUD.* WHAT DO YOU THINK?

"IN THE BEGINNING, THERE WAS NOTHING..."

SOMETIMES, IT FEELS LIKE BATMAN HAS BEEN WITH US FROM THE BEGINNING. LIKE HE'S *ALWAYS* BEEN THERE. LIKE HE ALWAYS WILL BE.

UNFORTUNATELY, IN RECENT MONTHS, WE'VE LEARNED THAT BATMAN, AS WE KNEW HIM, WAS AS HUMAN AS WE ARE. HE BEGAN, AND HE ENDED.

...AND THEN, THERE WAS BATMAN. AND THIS WAS GOOD.

HAHAHAHA

I'M KIDDING. BUT IN A WAY, I'M NOT.

BUT THIS PROGRAM, IT'S ABOUT MAKING BATMAN LAST *BEYOND* ANY ONE MAN. SO THAT HE CAN ALWAYS BE THERE FOR US. SO THAT HE CAN BE A PART OF THIS GREAT CITY.

SO WHAT ARE YOU GOING TO SAY?

I DON'T KNOW.

YOU WANT MY ADVICE?

*FIGHT* FOR IT.

...FIGHT FOR IT? GERI WOULD HAVE ME ARRESTED.

SHE MIGHT. EITHER WAY, THOSE PEOPLE OUT THERE...THEY'RE THE BOSS, RIGHT?

SO GO OUT THERE AND SHOW THEM WHO'S BATMAN.

IN OTHER WORDS, THERE MIGHT BE SOME WRONG TURNS ALONG THE WAY...

JULIA...LOOK BEHIND HER. IS THAT... OH NO.

...THERE MIGHT BE SOME DETOURS. BUT TOGETHER, WE CAN MAKE BATMAN BIGGER, AND BETTER AND--

GET DOWN!

EVERYBODY! GET DOWN! NOW!

ROOKIE! TAKE A KNEE!

WHIRR

WHAT THE HELL ARE YOU--

WAIT, WAIT, WAIT! HOLD ON A MINUTE!

VARIANT COVER GALLERY

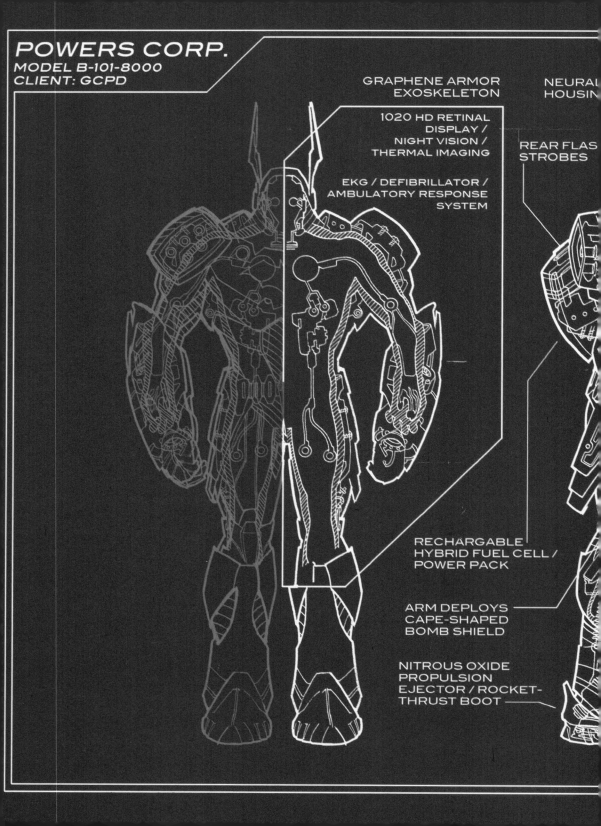

POWERS CORP.
MODEL B-101-8000
CLIENT: GCPD

GRAPHENE ARMOR
EXOSKELETON

NEURAL
HOUSIN

1020 HD RETINAL
DISPLAY /
NIGHT VISION /
THERMAL IMAGING

REAR FLAS
STROBES

EKG / DEFIBRILLATOR /
AMBULATORY RESPONSE
SYSTEM

RECHARGABLE
HYBRID FUEL CELL /
POWER PACK

ARM DEPLOYS
CAPE-SHAPED
BOMB SHIELD

NITROUS OXIDE
PROPULSION
EJECTOR / ROCKET-
THRUST BOOT

NCE

AUDIO INPUT /
DECIBEL DEFENSE

VOCAL PROJECTION /
AUDIO DEFENSE SYSTEM

RETRACTABLE
THERMO-RESIST
BLACKOUT VISOR

LIVE ROUND MAGAZINE
ARMOR PIERCE, SMOKE,
PULSE, TEAR GAS
EQUIPPED

SUIT HAS DIGITAL
CAMOUFLAGE
CAPABILITIES

SPINA-LINK
DIGITAL
CORE
PROCESSOR

MECH. VENTILATION/
EXHAUST MANIFOLD

100 PSI GRIP
FULL TACTILE
RESPONSE PROSTHESIS

ANTI-GRAV MAGNIVOLT
ALL-TERRAIN
STABILIZER

PROJECT
BATMAN

Retract

Retract

DC COMICS™

*"[Writer Scott Snyder] pulls from the oldest aspects of the Batman myth, combines it with sinister-comic elements from the series' best period, and gives the whole thing terrific forward-spin."*—ENTERTAINMENT WEEKLY

## START AT THE BEGINNING!

# BATMAN VOLUME 1: THE COURT OF OWLS

**BATMAN VOL. 2: THE CITY OF OWLS**

with SCOTT SNYDER and GREG CAPULLO

**BATMAN VOL. 3: DEATH OF THE FAMILY**

with SCOTT SNYDER and GREG CAPULLO

**BATMAN: NIGHT OF THE OWLS**

with SCOTT SNYDER and GREG CAPULLO

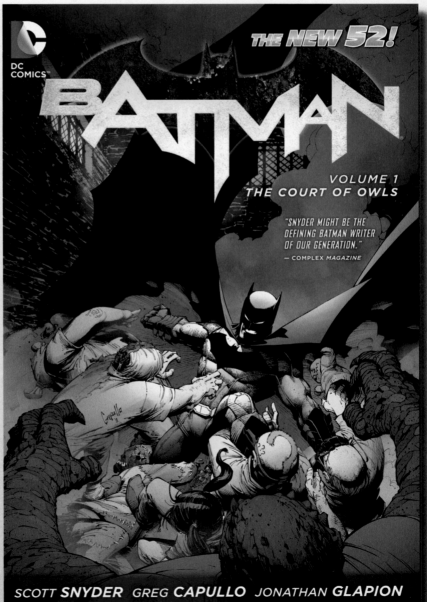

THE NEW 52!

DC COMICS™

**BATMAN**

VOLUME 1
THE COURT OF OWLS

*"SNYDER MIGHT BE THE DEFINING BATMAN WRITER OF OUR GENERATION."*
— COMPLEX MAGAZINE

SCOTT **SNYDER**   GREG **CAPULLO**   JONATHAN **GLAPION**

©2012 DC Comics. All Rights Reserved.

DC COMICS™

*"Combines the real world elements that have made the Christopher Nolan movies so successful with stylized visuals that only the comic medium can provide."*
—COMPLEX MAGAZINE

## MUST-READ TALES OF THE DARK KNIGHT!

# BATMAN
# EARTH ONE: VOL. 1
## GEOFF JOHNS & GARY FRANK

**BATMAN VOL. 3: DEATH OF THE FAMILY**

by SCOTT SNYDER & GREG CAPULLO

**BATMAN: KNIGHTFALL VOLS. 1-3**

**BATMAN: NO MAN'S LAND VOLS. 1-4**

DC COMICS™

DC COMICS™

"Groundbreaking."
—USA TODAY

"It's film noir in cartoon panels."
—VANITY FAIR

"Frank Miller absolutely revolutionized the Dark Knight
and his influence can be felt throughout comics, even
20 years later...true masterpiece of storytelling."
—IGN

FROM THE CREATOR OF *300* and *SIN CITY*

# FRANK MILLER
## with KLAUS JANSON

BATMAN:
THE DARK KNIGHT
STRIKES AGAIN

BATMAN: YEAR ONE
DELUXE EDITION

with DAVID MAZZUCCHELLI

ALL-STAR BATMAN
& ROBIN, THE BOY
WONDER VOL. 1

with JIM LEE

BATMAN: THE DARK KNIGHT RETURNS

FRANK MILLER
with KLAUS JANSON and LYNN VARLEY

DC COMICS™

"This is your go-to book."—ENTERTAINMENT WEEKL

"DETECTIVE COMICS is head-spinningly spectacular from to to bottom."—MTV GEE

# START AT THE BEGINNING!

# BATMAN:
## DETECTIVE COMICS
### VOLUME 1: FACES OF DEATH

**BATMAN:
DETECTIVE COMICS
VOL. 2: SCARE TACTICS**

**BATMAN:
DETECTIVE COMICS
VOL. 3: EMPEROR
PENGUIN**

**THE JOKER:
DEATH OF THE FAMILY**

Horsham Township Library